dedicated to all [illegible]

[illegible]

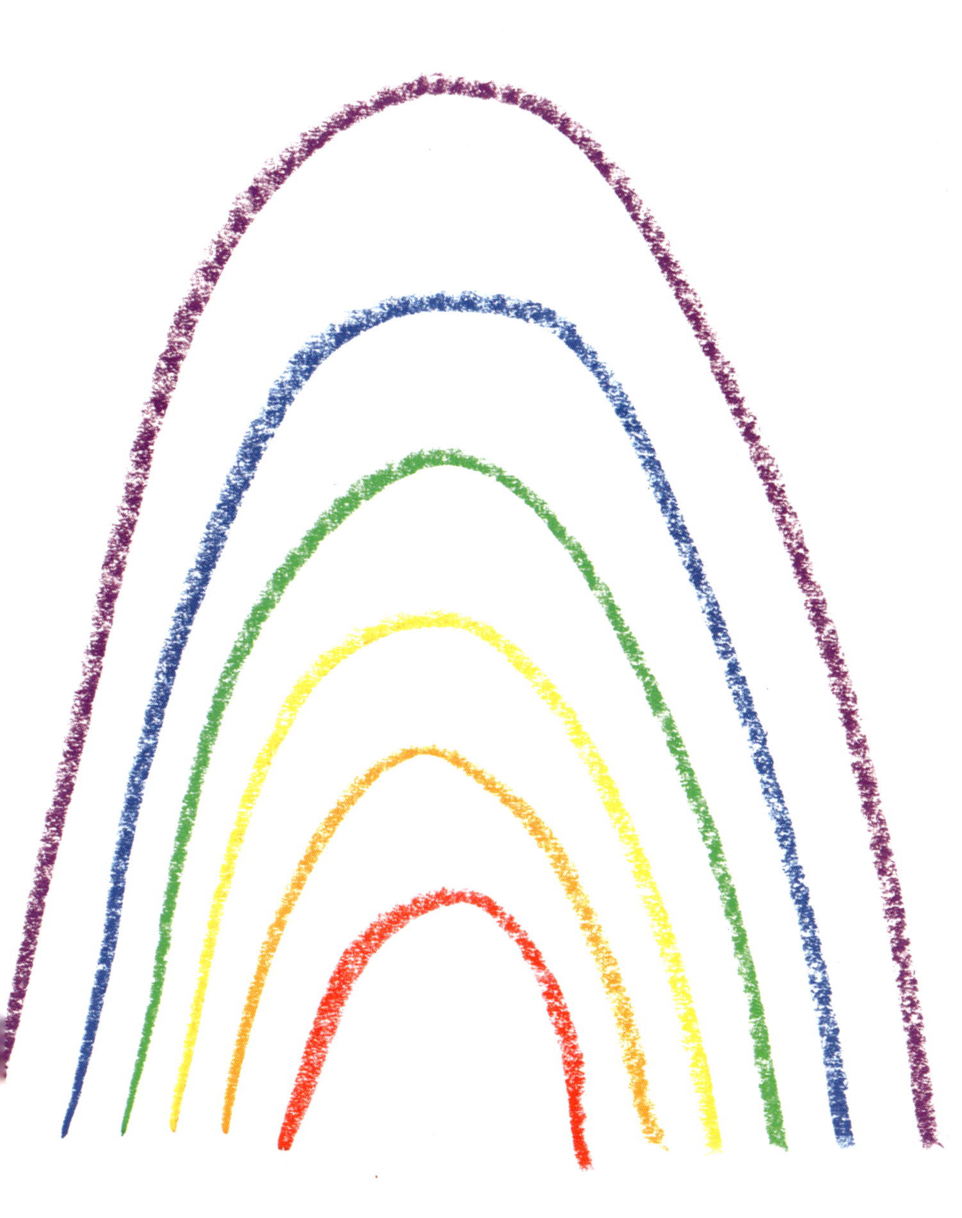

to whom it may concern

behind all the amateur eggs
i was plotting my debut
my existence was not vague
it was never up to you
mister geriatric pregnancy
i invite you to a duel
my mom gets it done
you silly, silly fool

How old are you?

Can I get pregnant?
How old are you?
Should I get pregnant?
How old are you?
Will I get pregnant?
How old are you?

I'm pregnant.
Wow, how bold of you.

the dance

9 months in your belly
36 hour labor
1 hour c-section
i'm hungry
you need to figure this out
i'm the leader

The Dance

9 months in my belly
36 hour labor
1 hour c-section
Can you please just wait a second
I need time to figure this out
I'm the leader

first love

i didn't know you'd be so pretty
i didn't know you'd be so kind
i didn't know you'd be so witty
i did know that you were mine

Meeting

I always wanted you
And now you are here
Did everything else disappear?

my perfect home

mommy you outdid yourself
your belly was great
but the nursery is even better
i have onesies for months
and big cozy layers
elephants dancing on the ceiling
i'm so relaxed
my home is perfect
together at last

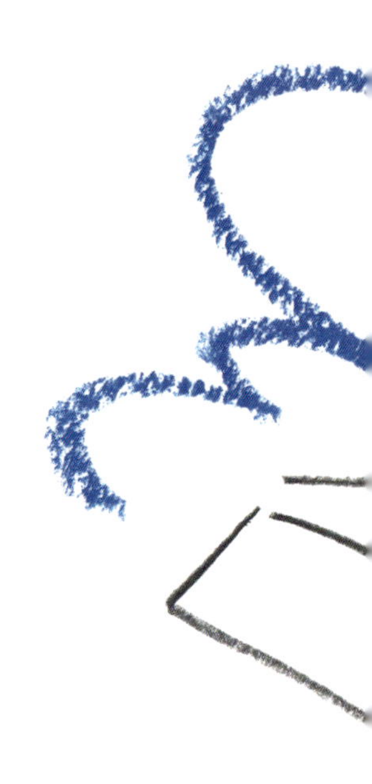

My Baby Bird

I bought every water wipe
Counted every sheep
Painted all the corners
'Til the whole room was complete
My dear baby bird
I'll listen to each peep
Dream big and go far
I waited long
To watch you sleep

sleep is overrated

this obsession with sleep
is low on my list
after all, we just met
let's snuggle and kiss

They say

They say when you nap, I should nap
They say when you poop, I should smile
They say when you scream, I should feed you
They say you'll grow up fast
Who the hell are "they"

poquito burrito

my arms are tucked in
i can't move my feet
i'm a stuffed up burrito
with no choice but defeat

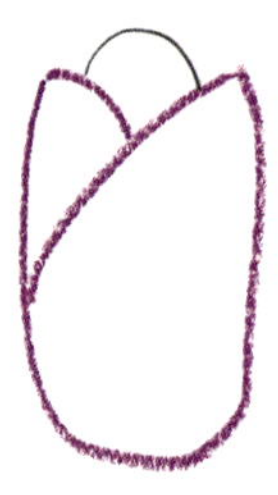

Tuck, roll and snore

This origami project
With an aim to protect
Guides me to tuck, fold and flip
Without any prep
Now...I close the door...
Goodnight, roll over and snore

hooters

rebrand this changing table
it's a mini spa
pour me a shot of breast milk
and get me to the bar

Diaper Dreams

If only this diaper protected all
From spills and disasters
Infections and diseases
To other private parts
I'm a mom with reasons
#diaperdreams

her skin

she's porous
feelings soak right through
she ages
weather stretches her coat
she touches
everything in her way
she holds me
like a cocoon at night

Your skin

It smells like innocence
It feels like bliss
It seems reminiscent
Of moments I'll miss

she loves me, she loves me not

i don't want to be an angry lover
but why would you choose that over me
i thought i knew you
c'est la vie

Pumping with options

Option 1: My tits explode
Option 2: My brain implodes
Option 3: I become a cow
Option 4: I learn how
Option 5: The world supports it
Option 6: I don't give a sh*t

i am

i'm a ball of fun
a mound of mush
with a smell so great
you kiss my tush

Sushi Shape

Pear or hourglass
Muffintop I'm not
The thought of cankles
Makes my stomach a knot
For all the things I could possibly be
A sushi roll stuck on chopsticks is what speaks to me

beginner baba

what is happening?
why are you scared?
is this cord on my belly
yours or mine
please figure it out
before i'm nine
i see the potential
but i'm getting cold
is water a good thing
i think i want clothes
please keep it calm
pull it together
just take me out
and get me a sweater

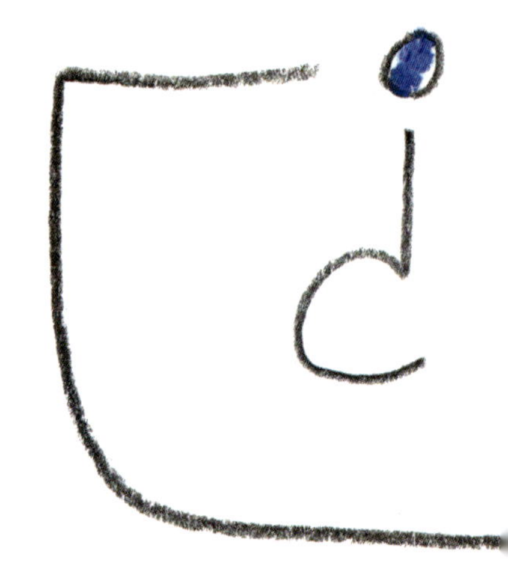

Bathing in bliss

I could have never foreseen
The joy of this routine
With every splash
I make my wish
Baba Time every night
Goodnight Moon, Goodnight Bliss

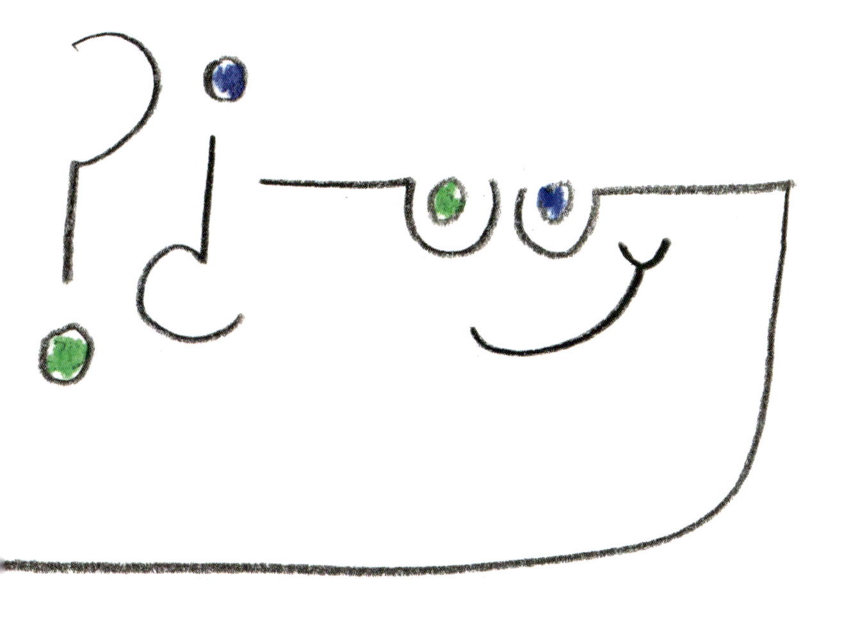

dr. obvious

wasn't i a monkey in my past
stop putting me on my tummy
get me on the grass
grown ups, i'm built to last

Modern parenting

Tummy Time, Tummy Time
In between rhymes
Sleep time, Sleep time
In between whines
Working, Parenting
Always negotiating
So much to do today and tomorrow
Is there extra time that I can borrow?

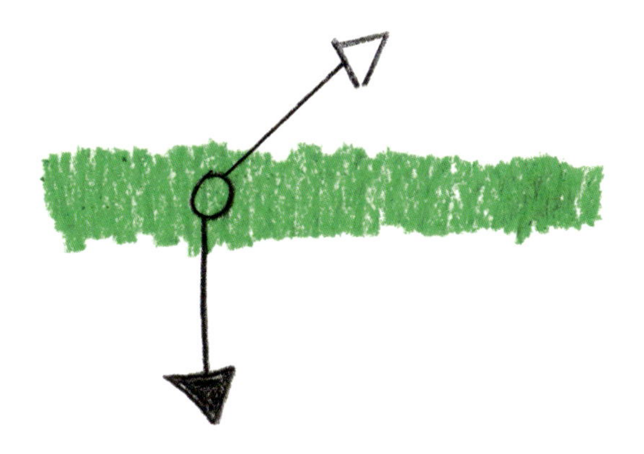

hint

i’m picking up
you don’t want me to talk
you’d rather have my gums rot

Pacifier

This is a magic tool
Do they have one for relatives too?

more cars, more problems

why would i want to sit in the back
the car in front of me is about to attack
turn me around and seat me in front
and put an end to this horrible stunt

Car Crib

Orange is the new black
The car is the new crib
Multitasking is the new way
Our world is global
Like it or not, our naps are mobile

self care

what do you mean
this concept is foreign
i've been looking out for myself
since the day i was born

Quiet Day

I need a quiet day
To sort through the grey
I need a quiet day
Will you be okay

I need a quiet day
For stress and despair
I need a quiet day
To find the repair

I need a quiet day
To bring the hope back
I need a quiet day
Before a panic attack

I'll take a quiet day
(Silence)

there are more

in your belly, i thought there was only you
i soon found out there are relatives too
i met a granny, a grandpa, a nini, a zadie
and friends who are family
in general, i am happy there are more
but to be honest, there are some i'd like to ignore

Family

Do I have too much?
Do I have too little?
What I need and what I want
Don't always meet in the middle
Everyone has issues
Party of One does too
There'll be tears and tissues
But I'll introduce you

you?, no... you?, no...you

if i smile enough i start to rock
then my insides fill up
with bubbles and dots
it's too much fun
mommy please don't stop
get me into trouble
until i drop

First laugh

What just happened
Freeze this moment
I'm beside myself
Beyond enjoyment
Take my heart
And make it a balloon
Better yet
Let's live on top of the moon

1, 2, thwee

1, 2, thwee
what a fun thing to be
you get to start every song
you get to count all the stars
you get to just be yourself
near and far

Milestones

Maybe you're a genius
1,2,3
What other child counts like that
Oh, all the others I see

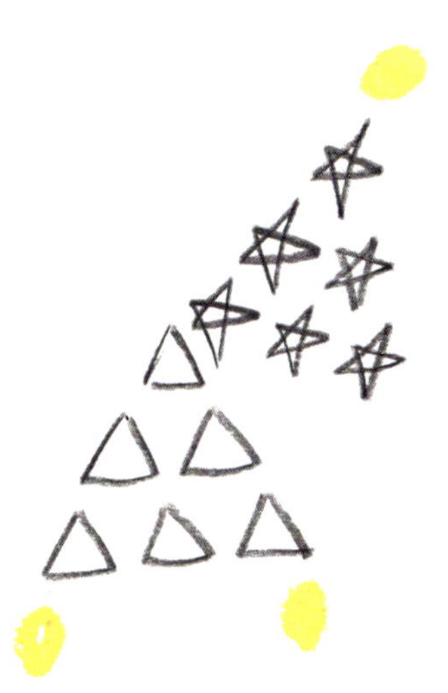

crummy mommy, happy mommy

you're my mommy
in any form
stay by my side
day and night
ride or die
crummy or happy
i want to hang with you

Pardon my Partum

Sorry I'm upset
Are you mad at me?
Sorry I'm scared
Do you have faith in me?
Sorry I'm confused
Do you still trust me?
Sorry I don't know
Do you want to hang with me?

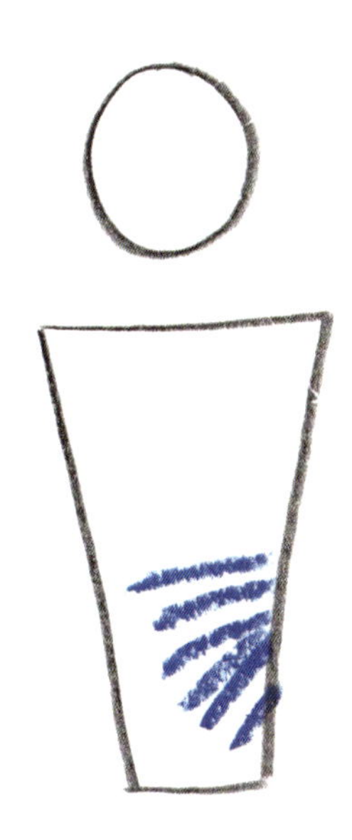

daddy

who needs insurance
who needs a doctor
who needs a lawyer
who needs friends
who needs food
who needs shelter
i don't need anyone
i have a daddy

You complete me

All the roles I never knew I needed
Wrapped into one
You've succeeded
For I have yet to come undone

i have sources

my mom seems wonderful
but you seem yummy too
do you have boobies for me?
i'm relentless
don't worry
my mom's not jealous

Help

I function like a workhorse
Love you more than the best nurse
Carry more than my big purse
Yet expectations are my worst curse
Do you have others you can coerce?

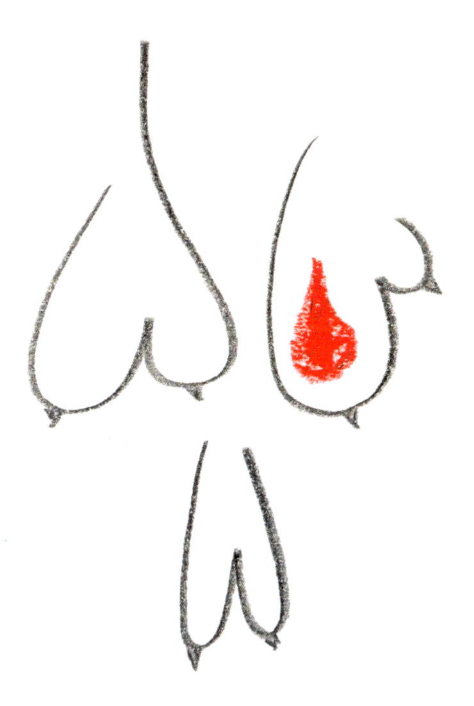

sweet noises or sweet dreams

am i back in your belly
or on a jet to the sky
i think i am ready
to say goodbye
wait wait...
hold me tight
does the noise machine kiss goodnight?

Magic Machines

When I turn you on
The night begins
When I turn you off
The morning starts
When I won't need you
I'll miss you my friend
The magic key to motherhood
Is stopping the machine
In my hand

age of wisdom

my blood is red
my heart is open
respect is earned
i too am human

Respect your elders

The world is perplexed
If gender leads to confusion
And religion leads to war
Is science a delusion
Are we apes or much more
It's all above my pay grade
But if I could make a bet
Respecting your elders
Makes the world better yet

my heart is yours

my hands are there for you to hold
please don't let them go
my feet are there for you to tickle
please don't walk away
my heart will be forever yours
just sleep with me today

Sleep talkin'

Cows go to sleep
So do you
Chickens take naps
So do you
Monkeys get tired
So do you
We're sayin' goodnight
I love you

mommy

ma
mama
mommy!

Mommy

This new name
Feels too old to belong to me
Generations yell it loudly
From the top of our family tree
I smile brightly
Baby, we made history

flavors, food, fun...oh my

i thought breast was best
but then i had an avocado
i thought drinking was my only option
but found chewing pretty awesome
i thought the fun would continue
but a big bite led to issues

Dealing

Reading led me to baby led weaning
Baby led weaning led me to feeling
That other than bleeding
Choking is high on the list
Of fears I'm feeding

taste test

sitting on this throne
being fed
putting food on my face
getting cleaned before bed
what did i do to get so lucky
i'll throw food across the floor
to my secret puppy

High hopes

Can the high chair come with a vacuum?
Can the new car come with a bathroom?
Can parenthood come with a classroom?

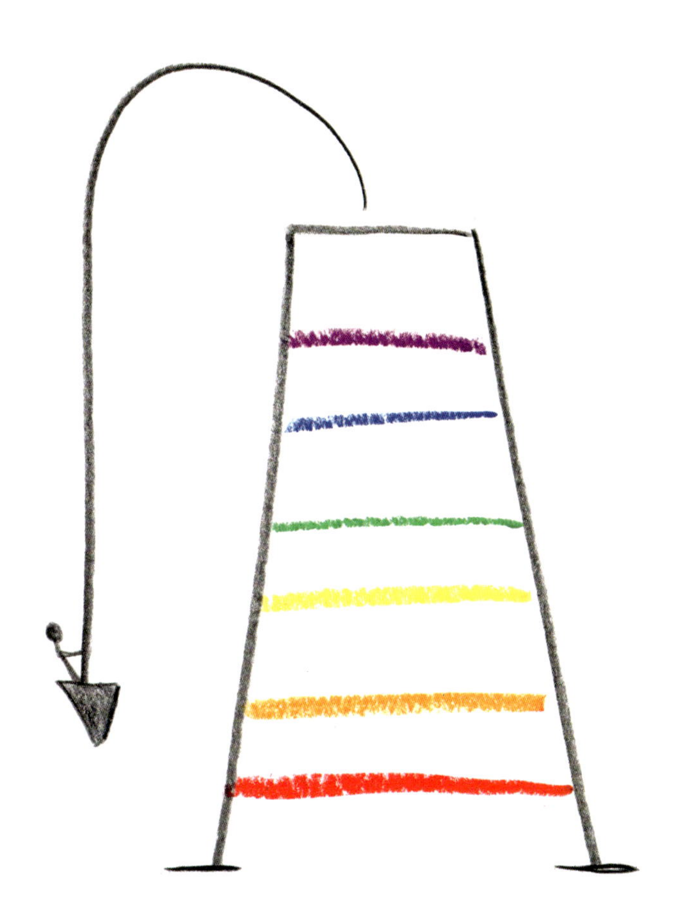

the good ole days

swing swing
in the sun
swing swing
i’m not done
love you mommy
childhood’s fun

My swing

I want to give you space
I love to watch you slide
I hope you can climb
Without me by your side
But can I guarantee your safety?
Please hold my hand and focus
My fear will swing to pride
If I try my hocus pocus

irony meet tyranny

let me get this straight
i’m next to your bed
in a baby jail
yet you’re complaining
about getting sleep
underneath your mound of sheets

Pack n' Pray

We have warning labels on common sense
Screen time junkies becoming therapists
All I can offer is real talk
Your Pack n' Play is my Pack n' Pray
Let's make it through the night then discuss the dismay

payment confirmation

i'm into the environment
you may need an intervention
amazon is not convenient
if my future is the payment

Global citizen

The birds are humming
But the talk is grim
It's all mind numbing
My options feel slim
The apocalypse is coming
I'll start recycling

what's your problem?

i can't walk
i can barely talk
let me feel some freedom please
next thing you know
you'll be a tiger mom
and put a mask on when i sneeze

Adultproof

I can't get up the stairs
Or into my cabinets
And the plugs seem dead to me
I don't even know who I am protecting
You or a baby octopus who's three

another mommy

another mommy
how dare you even ask
another mommy
wasn't hired for this task
another mommy
could be a hack
another mommy
may not have my back
another mommy
wasn't in our womb
another mommy
no thank you

The Tale of the Other Mother

The *Other* Mother
Doesn't get upset
The *Other* Mother
Doesn't skip a beat
The *Other* Mother
Has a perfect marriage
The *Other* Mother
Has time to eat
The *Other* Mother
Reaches her goals
The *Other* Mother
Cooks from scratch
The *Other* Mother
Is an idol
The *Other* Mother
Dresses with tact
The *Other* Mother
Has great legs
The *Other* Mother
Knows everything
The *Other* Mother
Doesn't worry
The *Other* Mother
Isn't me

happy day

everyone is smiling
i have cake all over my face
laughing in pictures
singing with grace
i hope everyday
we visit this place

Happy Birthday

We made it
All your limbs are attached
You have your vaccines
You're standing and reaching
For greatness it seems

potty mouth

this whole thing called poop
it's such a big deal
gossip starting after every meal
mom and dad speaking of it too much
i wish they'd be quiet and not rush
does the Christmas tree poop?
i sure wish it did
my wish for the holidays
is to crap like a kid

Doody Detective

Was it big or small?
An allergy?
Who knows...
When did your poop become my motherhood woe?

a walk in my shoes

being naked was a treat
now i have flippers on my feet
i vote land over sea
but bunions aren’t for me

Memory lane

I went from eating your toes
To dressing your feet
Can we save all these shoes
And every moment they bring

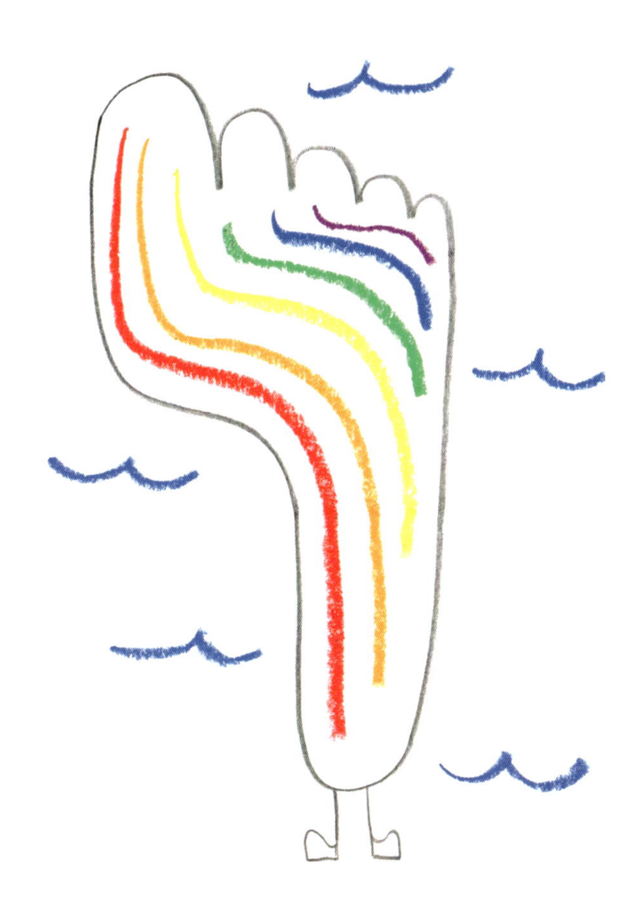

bounce for books

i feel like a joey
sitting in your pouch
thankfully i'm not at the zoo
i'm cozy on our couch
should i eat the book
or read the page
will you act it out
or sing it loud
can you use an accent
i can't contain
i'm your #1 sidekick
bounce my brain

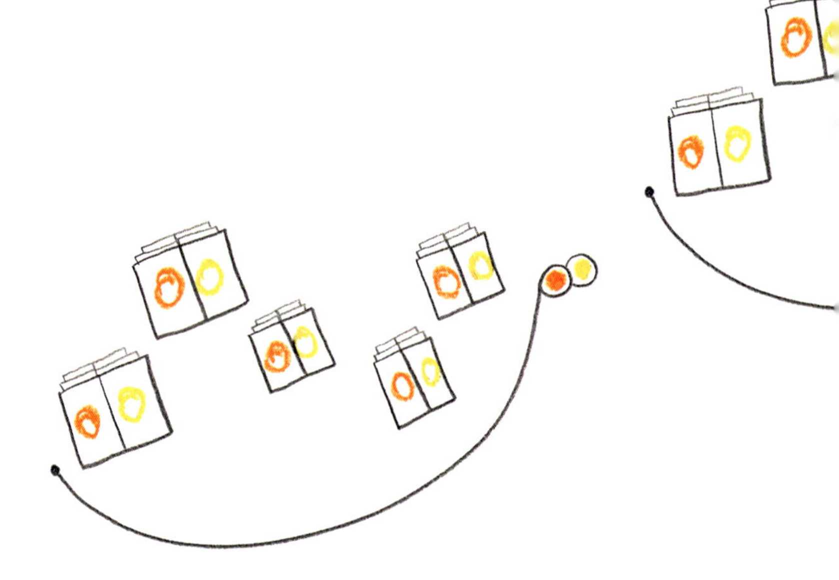

Our story

When you sit on my lap
My heart melts into yours
Let's share a story
And open doors

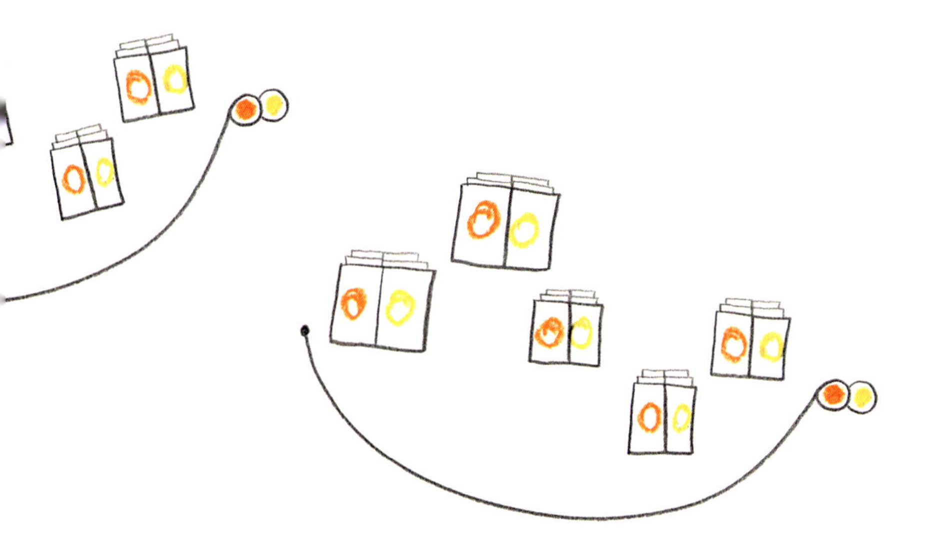

mommy and me class

i may pass on swimming
i'll go all in on drumming
yoga seems a bit intense
i'll try gymnastics
apply for tennis
but novels at this age are way too dense
truthfully the best activity
is time together, just mommy and me

The best activity

I want you to have it all
Basic stuff like playing ball
To big things
Like your own wedding
And in between
Maybe you'll show me
Things you want to do
With too many options
My ideas get limited
So let's go back to basics
Peek-a-Boo

luck

my mommy's mommy lives in the sky
she is everywhere my mommy goes
my mommy is so lucky
at dropoff she doesn't have to say goodbye

My mom lives in the sky

You woke in peace
You slept in peace

You sat in peace
You walked in peace

You listened in peace
You talked in peace

You were at peace
You are at peace

I miss you

"happy wife, happy life"

why do you get shotgun
on the road to happiness?
i'm the youngest one out here
and you're making a mess
choose a lane to drive in
or give me the wheel
confident driver, confident future
that's the winning deal

24/7

Does full-time worry
Make a full-time mommy?
Does part-time effort
Lead to half-full promises?
Does stay-at-home
Mean you're present too?
To all the mamas out there
Just do you

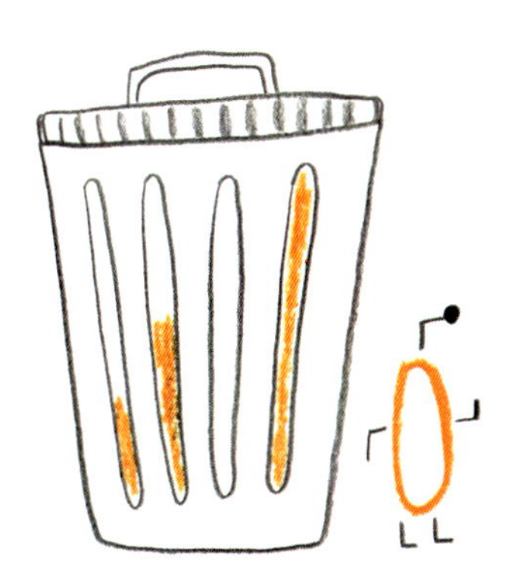

i want

i want everything
why wouldn’t i?
except the things i get when i cry
those things don’t seem to feel as good
so, all i want is a guaranteed mood

I accept you

Pie or crust
Lemon or lime
Chicken or egg
Rain or shine
Soccer or track
Quiet or loud
Moody or steady
I am proud

no

you say no
much more than yes
is this a reverse trick
to do less not more
you say no to my no
how confused are you
and imagine me, i’m only two

No, no, no

I promise there are so many things you can do
Just none of the things I don't want for you

what will i be?

supposedly i can just be
but where did that get anyone
i guess i'll crawl and walk
and then despite what you say
an expectation will be shared someday

You be you

Projection or Perfection
Seem to be the prototypes
I either see me in you
Or a scene for two
I just want you to be you
And keep me in your crew

"be nice"

why are you telling me to share
when i was here first
why are you telling me to listen
when it's not fair
why are you telling me to be nice
when i got hurt
why do i have to be their friend
when i don't want to be
why are you saying i should be strong
you expect too much of me

Cycle of Nice

When you dig really deep
You don't know who you'll meet
Some are sad
Others are fun
Just please set some boundaries
Before you come undone

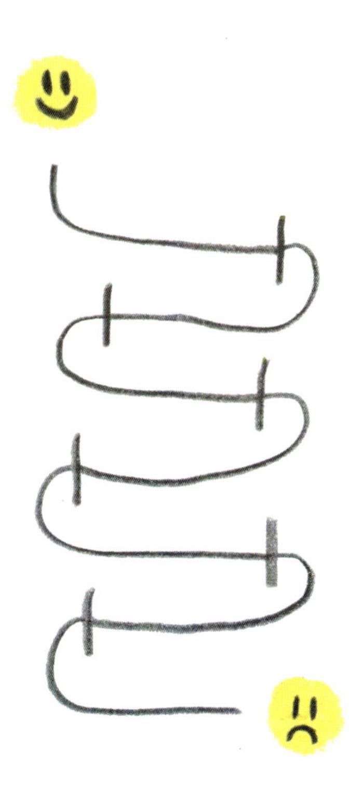

playlist

twinkle twinkle
kiss my cheek
itsy bitsy
hit repeat
head and shoulders
knees and toes
you have my heart
turn up the noise

Peek a Past

The childhood I think is gone
Comes back again with every song
The wheels on the bus always go 'round
The three little pigs always come down
From Old Macdonald to cock-a-doodle doo
A call back to the past was unexpected
Thank you

where is your belly button?

belly buttons are fun
do you want to see mine?
my mommy's is hard to find
it's above a pink bumpy line
sitting inside a donut design

My Belly

My belly is a pillow
My belly is life
My belly is an insecurity
My belly got cut with a knife
My belly is a story
Yours and mine

the world of i

i see so clearly in the world of i
i feel so easily in the world of i
i move so freely in the world of i
but when you show up
i want to cry

Tantrum

This moment for us
Revolves around you
You want it now
I could wait 'til tomorrow
You think I’m unjust
I assure you I’m not
Please let this pass
Stop hitting the pot

growing up

i woke up
i moved
i ate
i worked
i played
i went to bed
i do too much

Grown up

I woke up
I moved
I ate
I worked
I played
I went to bed
I don't do enough

are you sure?

you want another baby?
are you sure?
they may be wild
hard to tame
they may even be a bit insane
do we need another human?
this life is pretty good
expansion will affect our hood
ah forget it...
no one will listen to me
i'm a teeny dollop on the family tree
siblings can be pretty horrible
but i guess you're the one responsible

Another baby

After I stop breastfeeding
After I get my body back
After I become rich and famous
But before I'm too old
And before it's too late
Ah forget it...
Post amnesia
I'll just procreate

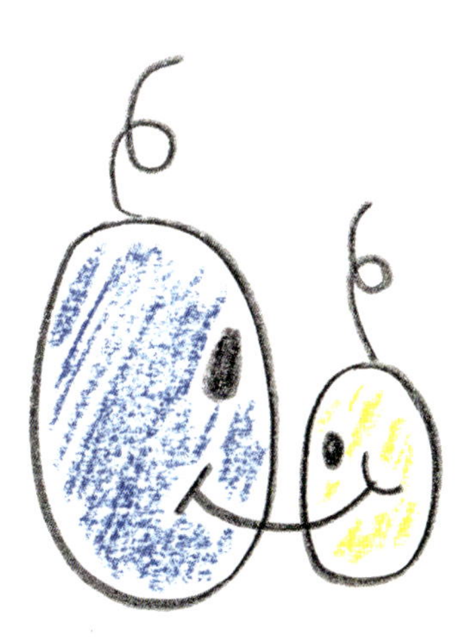

geniuses

i have a one stop shop
my parents know everything
but they get overwhelmed
about tasks like breathing

Wishing you well

Dear Kids,

We order plastic instead of composting
We surf the web rather than sleeping
We applaud speaking over listening
But our sky is your ceiling
If you just continue breathing

Wishing you well,
Humanity

my rain boots are happy

whenever it rains
people say a lot
about how the day goes
the have and have nots
but my yellow boots don't talk
they just beg for a walk
mommy tells me to nappie
but my rain boots are happy

Gifted and Talented

You wear rain boots on sunny days
Collect weeds instead of flowers
Hide rocks in my pockets
Stare at dead bugs for hours
You make friends with caterpillars
Run from sirens and cry
Build lego homes for critters
And love goodbyes
Your eyes see
What I cannot
I am thankful for
The gift I got

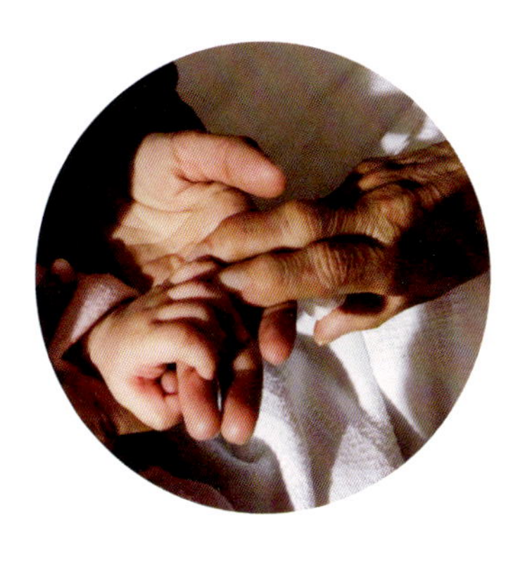

I love my mom and I love being a mom.

In 2019, I lost my mom the same year I had my first child.

I wrote and illustrated these poems to capture the precious, comical, ironic and fleeting moments of early motherhood.